C000182230

BRITAIN IN OLD PHO

LEICESTER
THEN & NOW

BEN BEAZLEY

SUTTON PUBLISHING

Sutton Publishing,
an imprint of NPI Media Group Limited
Cirencester Road · Chalford · Stroud
Gloucestershire · GL6 8PE

First published 2007

Title page photograph: Traffic duty at the
Clock Tower during the inter-war
years. (*Author*)

British Library Cataloguing in Publication Data
A catalogue record for this book is available from the
British Library.

ISBN 978-07509-4797-8

Typeset in 10.5/13.5 Photina.
Typesetting and origination by
NPI Media Group Limited.
Printed and bound in England.

Also by Ben Beazley

Wartime Leicester

Postwar Leicester

An aerial view of the city in 1973.
(*Courtesy of the Urban Design Group, Leicester City Council*)

CONTENTS

As late as 1955, many of the streets in the Hinckley Road district were still cobbled.
(*M. Ford*)

ACKNOWLEDGEMENTS

Without the assistance of a great number of people it would not have been possible to have compiled this album and I would like to take this opportunity to thank them both as individuals and groups for their help and generosity in sharing the material which is presented here.

I would like to thank Angela Cutting of the Community History Department at Leicester Library Services for allowing me access to their library photograph collection; Carl Harrison and the staff of the Record Office for Leicestershire, Leicester and Rutland for allowing me access to their material and all of their help in tracing and sourcing individual items; David Simpson for information on local railways and Derek Seaton for his encyclopaedic knowledge of civic history; Edna Welford for access to her late husband Eric Rourke Welford's collection; Gary Rossa and Justina Fewkes for their help in relation to R. Rossa & Sons; George Wilson of the Urban Design Group, Leicester City Council, along with Eric Selvidge and Geoff Fenn, for the fine collection of aerial photographs from their individual collections; Karen Ball of the Midlands Co-operative Society, Customer Services Department, for her help in relation to the area of High Street around the turn of the twentieth century; Malcolm Tovey for his generosity in sharing his unique collection of Fire Service photographs; Richard Everard, Chairman of Everards Brewery for access to the company's extensive photograph library; Stephen Butt and John Florance of BBC Radio Leicester for their help and assistance.

Others to whom my warmest thanks must go are: Boots Archives, Colin Chesterman, E. Norman, Fox's Confectionery, Geoff Forest, George Jordan, Janice Gunby, Leicestershire Constabulary, Margrid Ford, Mark Wood of Wood's Coaches, John Breen, Noel Haines, Philip Porter, Sir Jonathan North Community College, Suzanne Franklin, and Thomas Cook Archives.

Engineering workshop at Steel & Busks, Temple Road, 1960. *(S. Franklin)*

INTRODUCTION

O ver the last century the face of Leicester has continued to change dramatically due to many circumstances. The streets in the town centre were subjected to massive disruption at the beginning of the twentieth century when the Corporation installed an electric tramway system. A prime example is the High Street where between 1900 and 1903 many properties, including the ancient Huntingdon Tower, were pulled down to facilitate the widening of the road in order to allow the laying of tram rails.

During the Second World War, compared to many other cities, Leicester did not sustain a large amount of bomb damage. It was subjected on eight occasions to enemy attack – one night-time raid in particular on 19/20 November 1940 destroyed large areas of the centre and suburbs. This was certainly sufficient for the city planners to focus their attention on to how to redevelop the city centre for future generations. The first person to become substantially involved in this process was the city's engineer and surveyor between 1941 and 1964, John Leslie Beckett. It was he who devised what became known as the 'Fifty Year Plan', a project envisaging the restructuring of much of Leicester's road systems and many of its amenities. While Beckett's plans were sound, they took no account of historical values and required the demolition of much of the old town in the Southgates area. This meant the loss of much of the city's heritage. Among the new roadways that he laid down were the concentric ring roads that now circle the city, and the Southgates underpass cutting through the centre.

The next person to exert a major influence over future developments was Konrad Smigielski, a Polish-born architect who became the city's first Chief Planning Officer. During the ten years Smigielski spent in Leicester, between September 1962 and April 1972, he was responsible for the remodelling of the retail market place, the pedestrianisation of the Clock Tower area and the construction of the Haymarket Centre. His less successful ventures were a grandiose scheme to build an overhead monorail running across the city, an urban motorway from Belgrave to London Road, and a plan to build a forty-storey office block which would have been the tallest in the UK. None of these ever got off of the drawing board, and following a dispute with his management committee in April 1972 he cleared his desk and went into retirement.

Much was achieved especially in the years following 1945, however, when there was a will, locally and nationally (and providentially, government funds), to improve the lifestyle of the average person. Leicester City Council was not slow to become a part of this process, and areas of slum properties across the city, especially in the Wharf Street and Highfields districts, were cleared to be replaced by new inner city housing estates such as those at St Matthew's and St Peter's. On the outskirts building work proliferated. The Council's flagship New Parks Estate was the first post-war council estate to be completed, and private housing pushed the city boundaries ever outwards into the surrounding countryside. New commercial estates appeared on sites such as the old Braunstone Aerodrome.

One thing becomes very apparent in this process: as each generation comes of age, much of what they remember as children disappears, the horse is replaced by the motorcar, the tramcar by the bus, and people whose names are common at one time, fade into total obscurity fifty years later. If for no other reason than to keep some of these memories alive, the preparation of photographic albums such as this is a worthwhile undertaking.

Ben Beazley, 2007

1   The Old Town

L eicester as we now know it began to evolve soon after 1860 when the town's
two future main industries, the manufacture of hosiery along with boot and
shoe production gave it a strong industrial base. By the beginning of the First
World War the population had risen from 68,000 in 1861 to 227,000 in 1911.
The *Leicester and District Trades Directory* listed over 400 different firms either
directly involved in these two trades, or engaged in ancillary support work such as
knife-making, heel and lace production, and of course the very necessary
engineering works to provide machinery.

Seen as something of an architectural feat, towards the latter part of the
nineteenth century plans were laid for the construction of a New Town Hall which
was to be one of the most modern in the country. Designed by a locally-born
architect, Francis John Hames, and built by the London firm of William Brass, the
New Town Hall was officially opened Monday 3 August 1876. The old town hall in
Town Hall Lane, which had since 1495 accommodated the Corporation (and since
1836 the local police force and fire brigade), was left to its own devices for many
years until being adapted for use as a museum.

At the turn of the century the first major planned redevelopment work on a
large scale was carried out by the Town Council during the period immediately
before May 1904, when an electric tramway system was installed. This involved the
digging up of most of the roads coming into the borough and the entire area
surrounding the Clock Tower having to be excavated. Operating from a depot in
Humberstone Gate and a central garage on Abbey Park Road, routes radiating out
from the town centre were soon carrying passengers to and from the suburbs. One
particular thoroughfare to be affected was the High Street. To facilitate the passage
of the new tramcar system out from the Clock Tower to Hinckley Road and the west
side of the town, the entire length of the High Street need to be widened. This
involved the demolition and subsequent rebuilding, of large amounts of property.

During this period, the Market Place which, in an era before the concept of
supermarkets had become the norm, was the centre of commerce for both the town
and the surrounding county (or district as it was referred to). Local farmers would
come in with produce for sale, and housewives would undertake at least one weekly
journey into town to make purchases.

One other element played a key role in Leicester's development during this period
– the fact that the town was situated centrally in the heart of the Midlands. Typical
of the Victorian entrepreneurial spirit, the already existing canal system which
passed through the borough was quickly augmented by the new railway engineers

Market day in the years immediately before the First World War. At this time it was a common practice for farmers to bring their produce into the town to sell direct to the housewives who made the trip into town by tramcar once a week. From the straw hats and light dresses worn by the women in the picture it would appear to be mid-summer. *(Courtesy of the Community History Department, Leicester Library Service)*

and companies such as the LNER and the LMS were soon linking the town to the rest of the country from stations at Belgrave and London Road. This railway system remained an integral feature of Leicester and Leicestershire into the twentieth century when it was seriously curtailed by the closure of almost all of the local village railway stations by Dr Richard Beeching.

To continue the link with the fruit and vegetable trade which had been carried on since before the turn of the twentieth century, here we see the recently redesigned market place layout in the early 1970s. *(J. Gunby)*

Seen from the air in the summer of 1973 is the newly built Market Place with its solid canopy. The ground to the rear of the Corn Exchange has been cleared in readiness for the building of the new Fish and Meat Market. *(Courtesy of the Community History Department, Leicester Library Service)*

The women in this picture are much better dressed than would be expected of market traders, which indicates that they are probably Suffragettes running a market stall to collect monies for their cause. In the background at first-floor level is the sign of the now long-gone department store of Gee Nephew Ltd. *(Courtesy of the Community History Department, Leicester Library Service)*

The cheese market, seen here in the early years of the twentieth century. The market was held in Leicester Market Place for farmers from the outlying villages to bring their goods into town for sale. The Corn Exchange is on the photographer's left and we can see a very clear view of the premises behind the open market area. The firm of Turner & Co. traded as drapers, silk mercers, and general warehousemen, providing, according to their advertisements, 'a dépôt for convent and cottage industries'. First shown on this site in 1900, Francis Turner was trading as a silk mercer from premises at 54 Cheapside as early as 1870. Standing in the background gazing towards Cheapside, the statue of the Duke of Rutland was removed to the Castle Gardens in 1930. It was returned in August 1971 and placed a few metres to the right of where the old lady in the cloak is standing, near to the steps of the Corn Exchange. *(Courtesy of the Community History Department, Leicester Library Service)*

Viewed from the top of the Corn Exchange steps, a modern day view of the area where the cheese market took place.

Despite the ambitious advertisement placed in the *Midland Counties Advertiser* in October 1849, the Great Midland Emporium appears to have been a short-lived phenomenon. Trade directories for the time show no trace of the premises in the Market Place although its proprietor, J.J. Pratt, is earlier listed as owning a store in nearby Cheapside. *(P. Porter)*

The firm of Richard Morley & Sons began as Morley & Wright of Loughborough in 1828. Ten years later they moved into Cheapside on the site of the old fifteenth-century Angel Inn. Between 1888 and 1897 the company acquired premises in the Market Place and Cank Street. During the summer of 1952 much of the business was sold off to Maple & Co., of Tottenham Court Road, with only the Cheapside premises being retained. Along with the closure of many other city centre premises in the post-war years, Morley's announced in August 1962 that they were to cease trading at the beginning of 1963 and the Cheapside premises would be sold with vacant possession. *(Courtesy of the Community History Department, Leicester Library Service)*

Advertisement for
R. Morley & Sons from 1887.
(Author)

The old shop front of Morley's has now disappeared and all that is left is the small plaque at
first-floor level in the wrought ironwork bearing the company's initials. The alleyway to the
right of the picture is Morley's Arcade which leads through onto Gallowtree Gate. *(Author)*

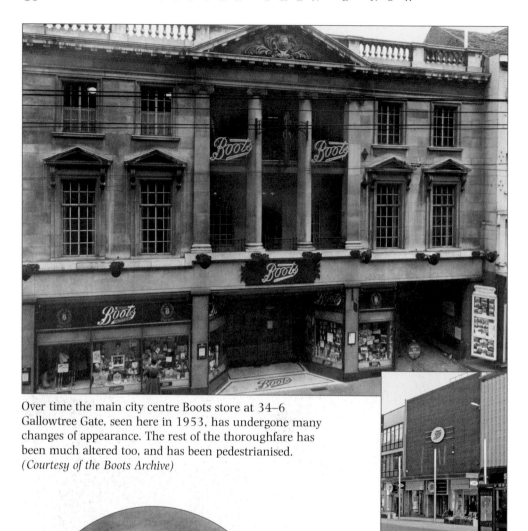

Over time the main city centre Boots store at 34–6
Gallowtree Gate, seen here in 1953, has undergone many
changes of appearance. The rest of the thoroughfare has
been much altered too, and has been pedestrianised.
(Courtesy of the Boots Archive)

The firm of Boots was begun in 1849 at
Nottingham by a Methodist couple, John
and Mary Boot, selling herbal remedies
among the poor of the city. Their son
Jesse was born in the Hockley district of
Nottingham in 1850. When he was ten
years of age his father died, leaving his
mother to run the family's small shop.
Leaving school at thirteen, Jesse went
to work in the business and became a
partner in 1871. From this point on,
trading as Boot & Co. Ltd., the company
continued to grow until by 1913 it had a
chain of 560 shops across the country, along
with a manufacturing site at Nottingham.
Knighted in 1909, Jesse Boot died in 1931 at the
age of eighty-one. *(Courtesy of the Boots Archive)*

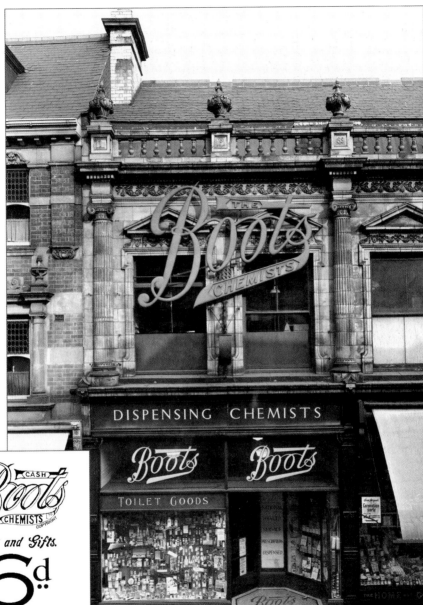

Opened in October 1924 Boots at 6 Cheapside was closed in about 1968. *(Courtesy of the Boots Archive)*

The New Town Hall was designed by Francis John Hames of Lincoln's Inn Court and built by the London firm of Wm. Brass & Co. Following the removal of the cattle market from Horsefair Street to Aylestone Road in 1872, work began on the New Town Hall in August 1874 and was completed during the summer of 1876 at a total cost of £52,911.

The removal of the Corporation from the old town hall in Town Hall Lane (now the Guildhall Museum), took place on August Bank Holiday Monday 1876, led by a procession of mounted policemen, decorated fire engines and the bands of the Volunteer Rifles and Yeomanry.

The absence of workmen and the presence of the lady standing outside of the main doors quietly surveying the site indicates that this picture was probably taken on a Sunday morning near to the completion date. In the background to the right is the Theatre Royal in Horsefair Street. At this time the clock had yet to be installed in the tower at the far right. It was originally intended that the building would be completed a year earlier but a series of industrial disputes delayed the work. In anticipation of this the date 1875 has been let into the stonework of the central ornate pedimental gable at roof-top level. (*Courtesy of the Community History Department, Leicester Library Service*)

Above, left: Paynes shop in the High Street, *c.* 1880. *(Courtesy of the Midlands Co-operative Society) Above, right:* Theophilus Payne is listed as a fish and game dealer in High Street as early as 1827. While it is probable that he traded from these premises at 44 High Street, the specific number at that time is not listed. Certainly in later years William Payne & Son traded from no. 44, which was on the left-hand side of the road between the Clock Tower and Cart's Lane. The earlier of the two pictures, with the nameboard clean and brightly painted, dates to a much earlier time than the second. Although there are two street doors adjacent to each other, the double front is all one premises. (Note the two rows of hooks at first-floor level over the doorways, used to hang game such as pheasants and rabbits for display. At Christmas these would have been laden with geese and turkeys). The second picture is much later – the board is faded and the lettering almost indistinguishable. Over the doorway of no. 42, almost indecipherable is the name P. Joseph. This refers to Philip Joseph who ran a furniture and house furnishing store from these premises. The public house at no. 46 was the Roebuck Vaults. Owned from the latter half of the nineteenth century by Meadows and Son, George Alfred Meadows, (the beginning of his name is clearly visible on the board between the first- and second-storey windows), held the licence between 1881 and 1890 which dates the picture to within that ten-year period. *(Courtesy of the Midlands Co-operative Society)*

After the loss of properties for the widening of the High Street at the turn of the twentieth century, a block between nos 40 and 60 disappeared completely, to be replaced with what was first termed 'the Electric Theatre' and later became known as the Cameo Cinema. Surviving as a picture house until the mid-1970s, it was converted for use as a Bingo Hall in the 1980s. *(Author)*

Photographed in January 2007, the block has once more changed dramatically, this time in favour of a complete rebuild. Completed in a style to fit in with the general appearance of the rest of the area, the site is now occupied by Habitat. (*Author*)

On a warm summer's day around the turn of the twentieth century, this group of Edwardian ladies stands outside John Annal's clothing shop at the corner of Cart's Lane. To the left is the junction of Union Street and High Street, with Richardson's boot and shoe shop prominently displaying its sign. Further along the street is the Huntingdon Tower. (*Courtesy of the Midlands Co-operative Society*)

Half a century later virtually the same scene on a summer's day in the mid-1950s. Watched closely by a schoolboy, workmen are repairing paving stones outside the Co-op building. Richardson's shoe shop has been replaced by the more famous Magnet Stores and Annals shop has now become the Co-op butchers. (*Courtesy of the Midlands Co-operative Society*)

Comparing this 2007 picture with the one taken during the 1950s, there have been many significant developments in the intervening half-century. In the far background, the block of properties, containing among other things the famous 'House of Bewlay' tobacconist shop, have been replaced by the Haymarket Centre and in the distance the tower of the BT telephone exchange in Wharf Street can be seen. The old-fashioned lamp standards with telephone connection points along the tops have disappeared and the ubiquitous yellow lines indicate that parking regulations have replaced the policeman standing by the kerbside. On the opposite side of the road, not only has the Magnet Stores at the corner of Union Street disappeared, but so has Union Street itself to be replaced by an entrance to the Shires shopping centre. The old Co-operative Society building is now Rackham's. (*Author*)

Before the opening of the Leicester Co-op's Model Dairy at Gimson Road, the horses for the company's milk and bread rounds were stabled at the Union Street headquarters in the town centre. (*Courtesy of the Midlands Co-operative Society*)

Despite the level of destruction taking place around it, the 'Family Fry Pan' at 106 High Street, owned by William Hallam, continues with business as usual. Seen from St Nicholas Street looking down towards the Clock Tower, the scale of the widening scheme can be fully appreciated. Buildings are in the process of being pulled down in readiness for the laying of the lines for the new electric tramway system in 1903. *(Courtesy of the Midlands Co-operative Society)*

A view from almost the same spot just over a hundred years later. On the far right, the premises of Mark Jarvis have replaced Hallam's 'Family Frying Pan', and the large curved dome of the Singer Building dominates the building line approaching Cart's Lane. *(Author)*

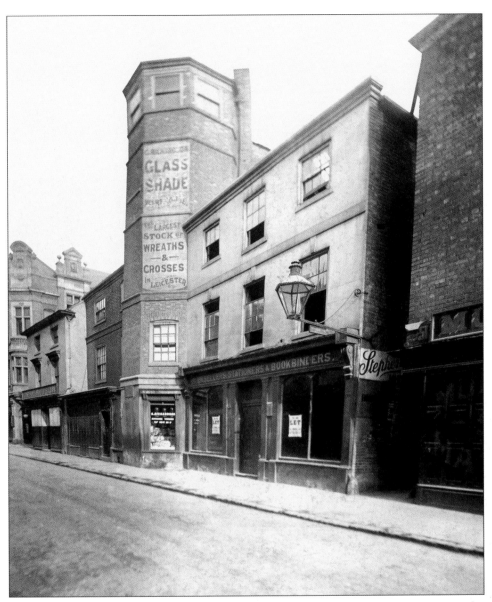

The High Street in 1902, closed in readiness for the widening process, preparatory to the installation of tramcar lines. In the centre, forming a part of George Richardson boot and shoe manufacturers' premises, is the old Huntingdon Tower which, built in 1569 during the reign of Queen Elizabeth I, formed part of the residence of Henry, 3rd Earl of Huntingdon. Over a period of time the tower saw a number of auspicious visitors including Mary Queen of Scots; King James I; and in 1642, Charles I. After its demolition, the site of the tower was identified by a simple plaque over the shop doorway built on the site.

At the far left of the picture stands the Co-operative Society building on the corner of Union Street. In the centre of the picture are the premises of Buck, Winks & Son, booksellers and printers. Next to the alleyway, Little Lane (surviving the forthcoming alteration work, Little Lane remained in existence until the area was once more developed by the building of the Shires shopping centre), is the hatters shop at no. 51 belonging to Ebenezer Murray. *(Courtesy of the Midlands Co-operative Society)*

With widening work under way, the premises of Richardson's, seen here just below the junction of Union Street, is well into the process of being demolished. *(Courtesy of the Midlands Co-operative Society)*

Following the rebuilding of the properties in High Street, a commemorative plaque stone was let into the wall at first-floor level on the site of the Huntingdon Tower. The small plaque (which still exists), fixed to the wall reads:

THESE PREMISES ERECTED IN 1903 ON THE SITE OF THE LORD'S PLACE BUILT IN 1569 BY HENRY 3RD EARL OF HUNTINGDON. HERE MARY QUEEN OF SCOTS LODGED IN 1586, KING JAMES 1ST IN 1612 AND HIS SON CHARLES IN 1642. THE FACE OF THE TOWER FORM NO PART OF THE BUILDING STOOD 8FT TO THE SOUTH OF THIS PLATE.

(Author)

At the turn of the twentieth century, this picture of High Street littered with horse dung (taken from a point between Cart's Lane and Highcross Street looking towards the Clock Tower), demonstrates just how narrow the roadway was before it was widened. In the centre left, the upper part of the impressive façade of the Co-op Building can just be made out, as can the Huntingdon Tower. *(Courtesy of the Midlands Co-operative Society)*

Taken some time between 1899 and 1903, this is one of the last photographs of the High Street in existence before the tramways were installed. At the left of the picture is Edwards wine and spirit store (originally also incorporating a chemist shop), which in later years became Lloyds Bank. Occupying nos 3 and 5 (Marlborough House) is the millinery and straw hat shop belonging to Emily Lovell, with next door to it J. Foster's grocery shop. In 1898, before Foster's took over, the shop was occupied by the Star Tea Company for a very short while, hence the legend at second-floor level advertising 'Dar Jeeling Tea 1/7d 1/5d'. On the far corner of New Bond Street at 2 Eastgates are Johnson & Co., who until just before 1900 traded as the 'Consumers Tea Company'. After moving to premises in the Market Place they continued to trade from 2 Eastgates as provision merchants. However, as the board over the shop was probably not altered, the picture cannot be dated to then – it is the absence of tramlines or overhead cables that gives a latest date of 1903. In the background along

the Haymarket from right to left can be seen the edge of Thomas Hayman's saddlery, then Burton & Sons photographers, followed by the White Hart Hotel. *(Courtesy of the Midlands Co-operative Society)*

Seen in 2007, the row of buildings has been completely changed twice, first to permit the widening of the road at the beginning of the twentieth century, then to allow for the building of the Shires shopping centre at the end of the century. During the initial changes, Edwards wines & spirits was replaced by the bank, and during the second, the entrance to the Shires replaced New Bond Street. *(Author)*

The opening of the Great Northern Railway's Belgrave Road station, 2 October 1882. For the next eighty years the line provided an essential commuter link for Leicester people travelling to all parts of the country. During the 1950s at the cost of a 10s return ticket, the most popular destinations for holidaymakers were the east coast resorts of Mablethorpe, Sutton-on-Sea and Skegness. Under the massive local rail cuts imposed by the Beeching Report, the decision to close the Great Central Line resulted in 200 staff at Leicester being made redundant in October 1964. *(Courtesy of the Community History Department, Leicester Library Service)*

The GNR sidings at Swan Lake Mills during the 1950s. At the bottom of the picture, busy with freight trucks and a locomotive making steam, is the Great Central locomotive depot, which was accessed from Marlow Road near to Narborough Road. The track running from top to bottom of the picture under Upperton Road and along the back of the houses in Western Road is the main line out of the city. The one crossing it at right angles is the Burton line. As yet the area of land adjacent to the River Soar is an undeveloped allotment site. *(Courtesy of G. Fenn; background information supplied by D. Simpson)*

An unusual photograph of a horse-drawn timber wagon having its axle weight checked on the old weighbridge at the junction of Soar Lane and Warrington Street. Alfred Lees, whose name appears over the door of the Ship Inn on the right of the picture, took the licence of the premises between 1922 and 1925 dating the picture to within this short period. The man in the plus-four trousers and cap who is peering under the chassis is the weigh clerk; the youth next to him, similarly dressed, is probably his assistant. By the turn of the twentieth century this scene was completely altered. Warrington Street had disappeared, as had the single-storey weighbridge building. A new pub of the same name is now set back from the roadway at the place where Warrington Street came into Soar Lane. Further along, Swan Street still exists with an original building on the corner, and a cobbled section of the roadway is still in existence. *(Top photograph: G. Fenn; right and below: Author)*

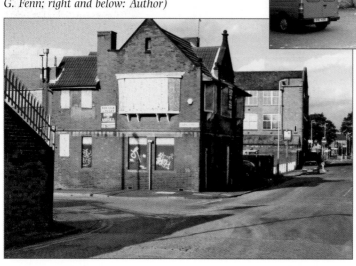

Not to be confused with the South African War Memorial (also in Town Hall Square and later moved from its position facing into Bishop Street to the corner of Horsefair and Every Streets), the memorial to the men who died in the First World War was unveiled by the Duke of Rutland on 28 June 1917. Initially the memorial carried the names of 2,129 Leicester and Leicestershire men who had died in the conflict. Space was left for additional names to be added later. This picture, taken from a postcard of the time is probably of the memorial being prepared for its unveiling, with the man on the steps adding the final touches to the work. Always intended to be of a temporary nature, the memorial was removed in 1925 to its permanent site on Victoria Park. *(Courtesy of G. Jordan; background information supplied by Derek Seaton)*

The old hall at Belgrave was built between 1709 and 1713 by Edmund Cradock, a wealthy hosiery merchant. At this time framework knitting was the staple trade of Leicester borough. After Cradock's death the hall itself became an hosiery centre under the auspices of the Vann family. In 1845 it passed into the hands of John Ellis, the railway entrepreneur responsible for bringing the railway to Leicester in 1833. The property now is part of Leicester's chain of museums. *(Courtesy of the Community History Department, Leicester Library Service)*

2 Early Twentieth Century

The early part of the twentieth century was for Leicester, a time of prosperity culminating in the four years of the First World War. With a firm industrial base established, in August 1914 war was declared, and there was initially a temporary dip in trade figures as, despite an enthusiasm to fight the Germans, an initial panic swept through most industrial and financial institutions across the country. This was followed in Leicester almost immediately by a general surge in production at all levels. With a government that was dedicated to 'business as usual', firms in the town joined the general clamour to obtain lucrative contracts to supply goods to the armed forces. The production of munitions was not confined to guns and shells, but included every aspect of trade that kept an army equipped and on the move. In the case of Leicester this included boots, shoes and clothing. A relatively small number suffered, the sequestering of horses and a large proportion of available fodder hit local blacksmiths, hackmasters and saddlers in the town along with farmers in the outlying districts, but in the larger picture they were a minority – most trades, and those employees fortunate enough to be designated 'essential workers', prospered.

The town was politically divided. In the summer of 1914 before August, there had been a lot of Suffragette activity in the county which rendered the women's cause somewhat unpopular among those opposed to universal suffrage. Showing a high degree of political skill the leader of the cause, Emmeline Pankhurst, informed the government that in support of the war effort, while the Suffragettes would still maintain their aims, all subversive activities would cease. In contrast one of the town's two MPs, James Ramsay MacDonald, adopted a vociferously anti-war stance throughout the four years of the conflict, leading to his becoming extremely unpopular both within the borough and nationally, and resulting in more than one episode of civil disturbance at open-air meetings, usually held in the Market Place.

Before the passing of the British Military Service Act in January 1916 (which brought in compulsory conscription), all of the British Forces were either pre-war regulars or volunteers who had joined up to fight the war. During the early months, local men flooded to enlist and among these were hundreds in the employ of the Town Council – firemen, policemen, teachers, tramways employees, gas and electricity workers – all of whom, in order to demonstrate the council's support for the war effort, were kept on full pay. As the war dragged on past the initially

By the outbreak of war in 1914 the Leicester Borough Fire Brigade, under the leadership of Henry Neal, had become one of the most modern in the country, having been among the first to mechanise its fire-fighting fleet. *(M. Tovey)*

anticipated few months this was to create a massive post-war financial problem for the Corporation.

Apart from the commercial implications of Leicester being at the centre of the country's transport network, there was another significant advantage, it was ideally situated to receive casualties. Converted in 1914 from the derelict site of the old County Lunatic Asylum into a modern military hospital, the future university buildings on Victoria (later University) Road soon became the 5th Northern General Hospital which was one of the largest of its kind in the Midlands. It later included the old Workhouse Hospital (now the Leicester General), and a host of smaller units throughout the county.

The ultimate accolade for the town's contribution to the war effort came on 10 June 1919 with a visit to the town by HRH King George V and Queen Mary, when the town's recent mayor Jonathan North was knighted and Leicester was granted city status.

During both world wars many of those who volunteered to join up were not of English origins. Seen here at the beginning of the First World War are three young Italian men who had come to live in Leicester soon after the turn of the twentieth century. On the far left of the picture is Rafael Boccarossa (the proprietor of R. Rossa & Sons, ice cream manufacturers), who served throughout the war in the South Staffordshire Regiment, with his two companions, Giuseppe Defazio and Antonio Rossi. *(J. Fewkes)*

Women's suffrage was a major issue at the time of the
First World War and many large meetings such as this
one in the Market Place resulted in disorder.
(Courtesy of Leicestershire Record Office)

During the summer months immediately before the First World War, the Suffragette movement under the guidance of Emmeline Pankhurst (1858–1928) was particularly active in the Leicester area. On 2 June an attempt was made by women from the movement to set fire to Nevill Holt, the home of Sir Bache Cunard at Medbourne, and on 12 July they succeeded in burning down Blaby railway station. In the interim period amid other activities such as holding political meetings in the town centre, a group of Suffragettes set up a stall in the Market Place near to the White Swan public house, selling cakes and confectionery to gather funds for the Women's Social and Political Union. An angry crowd of objectors gathered and disorder resulted which had to be broken up by a contingent of police from the nearby Town Hall police station. Displaying a high degree of political astuteness, as soon as war was declared in August 1914, Mrs Pankhurst came to an agreement with the government that the WSPU would cease their activities for the foreseeable future in return for the release of all Suffragettes in British prisons in order that the organisation could support the country's war effort. (*Courtesy of Leicestershire Record Office*)

During the four years between 1914 an 1918 Jonathan North (1855–1939) was one of the central figures in carrying Leicester through the vicissitudes of war. An agreement was reached at an early stage that there would be no local elections for the duration of hostilities which resulted in North holding the position of mayor for the duration. In 1917 with the end of the war imminent it was decided that he should now be succeeded by a local tobacco dealer, Percy Litton Baker. Unfortunately Baker died and the office was not rotated until the following year, just before the armistice in November 1918, when Walter Lovell became mayor (the title of lord mayor was not adopted until 1927). In June 1919 when the king conferred upon Leicester city status, he also knighted Jonathan North at the De Montfort Hall. (*Courtesy of Sir Jonathan North Community College*)

Near to the junction with Belvoir Street, while retaining its first-floor aspect, the shop at 14 Bowling Green Street has at street level changed considerably over the years. It has had an entirely new frontage and the front door has been moved to the opposite side of the premises. *(Author)*

In 1915, this group of Leicester men serving in the Army Service Corps were photographed before leaving for France. Back row, left to right: A. Hubbard, G. Drake, R.B. Willis, W. Needham. Middle row: C. Hardesty, J. Briggs, W. Harris, A. Lockwood, W. Cowley. Front row: A.R. Hall, J. Rouse, R. Clowes, T. Moore, W. Rosevear, W. Fairey, W. Fieldsend. *(Author)*

Many men who initially enlisted for service in local regiments were quickly transferred to units to which their backgrounds were more suited. One such was Alexander William Burton. A Scotsman born in 1886, Burton was already a serving officer in the Leicester Borough Police when he enlisted in the Leicestershire Regt, as Private 6376 on 22 March 1915. After basic training he was transferred to the Mounted Military Police and served throughout the war in France. Following his discharge from the army in June 1919, he returned to his former occupation, in which he served as a sergeant until retiring in April 1937. (E. Norman)

On demobilisation soldiers were issued with a form Z.21. They were also given a twelve-month insurance policy to vouchsafe them against unemployment. The basis of this measure was to insure soldiers coming back from the war against hardship during the first twelve months after their discharge. Unfortunately, based on the premise that historically officers had always been gentlemen of independent means, this facility only applied to NCOs and other ranks. Failing to take into account that a huge number of enlisted men had been given battlefield promotions, this omission resulted in a great deal of hardship for many ex-officers. (E. Norman)

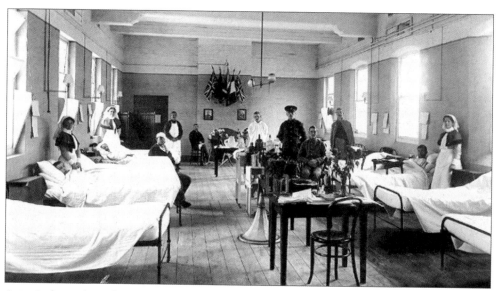

A typical ward at the 5th Northern General Hospital on what is now University Road. Utilised as a hospital from the outset of the war, the old County Lunatic Asylum (later to become Leicester University), the 5th NGH quickly became one of the largest war hospitals in the Midlands, taking casualties direct from convoy trains which came up from the south coast to the LMS railway station at London Road. *(Courtesy of Leicestershire Record Office)*

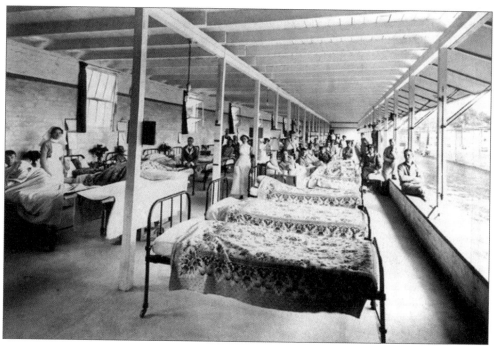

A new innovation at the 5th NGH in relation to dealing with men who had been gassed was to construct timber-framed open-air wards. In the summer these were very cool and airy, but in the winter bitterly cold. In the years up to and after the Second World War, these buildings were to serve as classrooms for many generations of pupils attending the Wyggeston Boys' Grammar School on the site. *(Courtesy of Leicestershire Record Office)*

Unnoticed today by the majority of passers-by, the residential home for the Institution of Trained Nurses at 73 Aylestone Road was built on the corner of (what is now) Filbert Street East and Aylestone Road in 1880. An Institute for Trained Nurses was first set up in the town in July 1866, following the engagement four years previously of three nurses from St Thomas's Hospital in London. The role of these women was twofold – to provide private nursing facilities for payment, and also to work among the poor. By December 1874 the institute had progressed to the stage where it could supply nurses to the Royal Infirmary. During the First World War the premises were leased to the War Office for billeting purposes. (*Author*)

Rutland Street fire station decked out with flags and bunting in celebration of the armistice being declared in November 1918. The banner surmounted by Britannia flanked by two lions reads 'Peace after Victory'. *(M. Tovey)*

HRH King George V reviewing the Guard of Honour (2nd Battalion Leicestershire Regiment), on Victoria Park. *(Courtesy of Leicestershire Record Office)*

On Tuesday 10 June 1919 HRH King George V and Princess Mary paid a visit to Leicester in order to confer city status upon the borough. Part of the proceedings included a marchpast of troops and other organisations from across the Midlands, which was reviewed by the king on Victoria Park. Such was the size of the parade that it took three-quarters of an hour to pass the saluting platform. Included in the ceremonies was the knighting of Jonathan North in the De Montfort Hall. *(Courtesy of Leicestershire Record Office)*

The events at Victoria Park were followed by a visit to the factory of Taylor, Taylor and Hobson in Stoughton Street. On leaving the premises the royal party travelled by open carriage down Sparkenhoe Street past the workhouse and over Swain Street Bridge en route to the railway station. *(Courtesy Leicestershire Record Office)*

COUNTY BOROUGH OF LEICESTER.

POLICE NOTICE.

AIR RAIDS.

The public are requested to make themselves acquainted with the following instructions with regard to the steps that will be taken in case of raids by hostile aircraft. They are earnestly asked to assist the Authorities by remaining calm, and by willingly and strictly complying with these instructions. They can greatly assist in safeguarding the Town by always strictly observing the Lighting Orders, and using the darkest curtains they can obtain.

Should it become known that hostile aircraft are approaching the neighbourhood, the following steps will be taken:

HOOTERS.– Steam hooters will be blown for a period of five minutes (if safe to do so). This warning will consist of a succession of five blasts - four short ones, followed by one long one.

As no steam hooters are now sounded after 4-0 p.m., the alarm may be recognised when a hooter is heard in the evening.

TRAMS.– The electric trams will be stopped immediately, and remain stationary until all danger is believed to be passed.

GAS.– The gas will be reduced to a minimum, and householders are earnestly requested to extinguish what light remains, taking great care to turn off the taps at the gas jets and the meter, to avoid danger in case of fire, or of explosion or suffocation after the pressure is restored.

ELECTRIC LIGHT.– The electric light will be gradually reduced to a minimum, and in this case also the public are requested to switch off what light remains.

FLASHLIGHTS.– The use of flashlights at such a time is strictly prohibited.

MOTORS AND OTHER VEHICLES.– Drivers must reduce their lights as low as possible, and proceed at a walking pace, and with the greatest caution. They must stop if requested. Motor horns must not be sounded unless absolutely necessary to avoid accident.

The Police have had strict instructions to report any driver who disobeys this Order.

If the drivers of vehicles are not bound to proceed they are requested to draw into side streets, extinguish their lights, and remain stationary. It should be borne in mind that the position of a town is likely to be located by the noise of traffic.

PUBLIC.– The public are strongly advised to remain at home. The windows and doors of the lower floors should be closed to prevent the admission of noxious gases in case of poisonous bombs being dropped etc. A supply of water or wet sand should be kept ready so that a small fire could be promptly and effectively dealt with.

FIRE ALARMS. Inhabitants should ascertain the position of the nearest Fire Alarm.

STREET LAMPS.– Householders opposite street lamps that are lit are requested to assist by turning them out.

SPECIAL CONSTABLES, Auxiliary Firemen, St. John's V.A.D., Citizens Training League, and other bodies, should assemble according to arrangements in force.

H. ALLEN,

14th February 1916   Chief Constable

After both wars celebrations were held to commemorate the armistices. These children are in fancy dress for a street party at the end of the First World War. Visible in the background on the counter of the ice cream van is a placard with the word 'Victory'. *(R. Rossa & Sons)*

3   Fire Brigade & Police

A piece of legislation enacted in 1835 – the Municipal Reform Act – brought about two seachanges in the lives of those living in Leicester. First, it entitled all male ratepayers to a vote in local council elections, which was to deliver a crushing blow to the existing Corporation. Previously only freemen of the town had been entitled to vote, a fact that had enabled the council to closely control elections, and to ensure that once in power it was almost impossible to dislodge its members from their controlling position. The result was that for many years prior to the passing of this Act the Tory-dominated local authority had become venal and corrupt. Subsequent to the Act coming into force in September 1835, an early local election removed the standing Town Council and replaced it with a body of businessmen (predominantly Liberal in persuasion), who had the town's best interests at heart.

From this point onwards the administration of the borough was put onto a much more positive footing and monies were spent to better the existence of Leicester's inhabitants.

The second effect of the new Act was that it required all newly appointed councils to establish police forces. While many authorities were somewhat laggardly in implementing this requirement (many took several years), Leicester was not, and within a few months, in January 1836, a police force under Inspector Frederick Goodyer, comprising five sergeants, and forty-five constables had been appointed.

In common with all of the other newly created forces across the country, Leicester Borough Police had the dual role of being responsible for both law enforcement and fire-fighting. Crews of constables were given the responsibility for attending any fires in the borough, and thus an embryonic fire brigade was formed. The two units continued to work side-by-side for just under thirty-six years until in December 1871 the Leicester Borough Fire Brigade was created as an autonomous organisation.

In 1909 with the arrival as Chief Officer of Henry Neal, a former Naval Engineer, the Brigade began to concentrate on mechanisation and by the outbreak of the First World War was one of the most modern and well-equipped in the country, with motorised engines and on-street fire alarms connected by the relatively new medium of telephone to a central control room.

For its part the Borough Police Force also evolved, and from its headquarters in the New Town Hall (opened in 1876), established branch stations at Sanvey Gate,

Firemen based at the North Evington fire station in Asfordby Street, 11 August 1902. The officer is George Law who was the officer-in-charge of the station. His living quarters are in the background. On the glass of the street gas lamp are the words 'Fire Station'. Opened in December 1899 the station was shared by the Police and Fire Brigade. Sadly, the horse in the shafts of the escape 'Bay Horse Charlie' met with a fatal accident a few months after this picture was taken. Returning to the station from a roof fire in nearby St Saviours Road he bolted, and attempting to jump a garden gate and wall became impaled on the spikes of a set of iron railings. *(M. Tovey)*

Belgrave, Woodboy Street, North Evington (where it shared a station in Asfordby Street with the Fire Brigade) and Queen's Road.

Both services started together in what is now the Guildhall in Guild Hall Lane before moving to the New Town Hall where the police remained until 1933. The Fire Brigade set up their headquarters in Rutland Street during the last decade of the nineteenth century and moved once more in 1927 to Lancaster Place.

When it came into being under the management of the Corporation's newly appointed Watch Committee in January 1836, the Leicester Borough Police Force also had responsibility for the fighting of fires in the town, and consequently a fire brigade section was created within its ranks. It was an uneasy marriage: fire officers held police ranks and as such often interfered in the day-to-day activities of constables. This situation was brought to a head on the retirement in 1864 of Henry Scott who had been Superintendent of the brigade since its inception and the appointment in his place from the London Fire Brigade of George Clamp. Given the rank of Police Inspector, Clamp proved to be a shadowy and controversial figure. For the next eight years until his dismissal in April 1872, Clamp was in conflict with police and public alike attracting numerous complaints concerning his overbearing manner and heavy drinking. On more than one occasion his drinking habit resulted in his arrival at the scenes of fires in a state of intoxication. The final embarrassment to the Watch Committee came late in 1871 when Clamp was charged before the magistrates with theft of some shallots from a local beer house. Although the allegation was not upheld it was decided that he should go, and his contract was terminated in April 1872. The affair was the catalyst for the splitting of the Police and Fire Brigade, and from December 1871 Leicester Borough Fire Brigade became an organisation in its own right. (G. Forrest)

Soon after becoming Chief Fire Officer, Henry Neal instigated a system of 'on-street' fire alarms linked directly to the Central Station in Rutland Street. In November 1914, three months after the outbreak of war, he negotiated with the Watch Committee for the Borough Police to use these at a shared cost. Some firms such as the British United Shoe Machine Company, W & A Bates of St Mary's Mills, and the Imperial Picture Theatre in Green Lane Road, were connected directly into the system at a yearly cost of £2. By January 1917 there were fifty-three such installations. *(M. Tovey)*

An early addition to the Borough Fire Brigade's motorised section, this new Merryweather pump is being demonstrated in July 1913 to members of the Borough Council at the side of the canal in Painter Street. *(M. Tovey)*

From the time that the police force and fire brigade were established in 1836 until fire brigades throughout the country were nationalised during the Second World War to create the National Fire Service, Leicester Borough and City Fire Brigade were responsible for providing the citizens of Leicester with an ambulance service. *(Top: M. Tovey; bottom: N. Haines)*

Leicester Borough Fire Brigade and Police Force were part of one organisation from its inception in January 1836 until December 1871 when the two organisations became separate entities. The Fire Brigade was based at the New Town Hall in Horsefair Street from 1876 until August 1892 when it moved into the premises in Rutland Street. At the time when this picture was taken (between March 1909 and February 1910) the brigade numbered eighteen permanent firemen (this was increased at the end of the year to twenty-four), of which sixteen were based at the Central Station in Rutland Street and 2 at North Evington. Attached to the brigade were a further thirteen Auxiliary Firemen (volunteers) who would turn out if needed. Back row, left to right: Frank Roberts, Sam Solomon, Dan Essam, Bob Topley, Abe Hincks, Arthur Ward, George Southam, Frank Griffin, Thomas Howe. Middle row: Alf White, Arthur Wright, Charlie Yates, Arthur Cole, Joe Goode, Harry Beaver, Harry Harrison, Tommy Knight, Billy Clarke, Andrew White, Walter Sturgess. Front row: Jack Potter, Walter Parker (Coachman – OiC Stables), George Law (3rd Officer), Fred Law (2nd Officer retiring), Henry Neal (Chief Officer), Jack Kinder (2nd Officer, newly appointed), Ted Smith (Sgt/Station officer), Billy Ames, Ted Howe. (*M. Tovey*)

Taken sometime between the wars, this posed yet informal photograph (there are no officers present), gives a charming and relaxed view of a group of firemen at the rear of the main headquarters in Rutland Street. One man in particular is of interest. Standing third from the right on the back row is Abraham (Abe) Hincks, who died suddenly in the fire station at Asfordby Street on 15 February 1937 at the age of 52. At the time he was serving as the District Officer at North Evington. For many years afterwards there were unexplained sightings in the building which led to the rumour that the station was haunted by his ghost. *(M. Tovey)*

Originally a naval engineer, Henry Neal joined the Grimsby Fire Brigade at the turn of the century in 1901 as Chief Engineer, becoming Chief Officer in 1903. Six years later he moved to Leicester as Chief Officer of the Leicester Borough Brigade. During his career at Leicester, which lasted until his retirement in 1937, by revising all of the underground water supplies and the introduction of mechanised vehicles, Neal was responsible for the foundation of what was to become the modern Leicester Brigade. (M. Tovey)

When he died on 7 April 1987 at the age of 104, Walter Sturgess was the oldest surviving member of the Leicester City Fire Brigade. Born on 10 March 1883, Sturgess began his career as a fireman when at the age of twenty-six on 24 October 1909, he joined the Leicester Borough Brigade. He served in the brigade for the next thirty years, and was promoted in January 1930 to the rank of Station Officer at a salary of 97s 6d a week before retiring in October 1939. (M. Tovey)

Walter Sturgess's son, also named Walter, also served in the City Fire Brigade and rose to the rank of Station Officer. He is seen here in 1937, nearing retirement himself. (M. Tovey)

With almost forty years' service as a fireman, Walter Parker was the longest serving officer on the Leicester Brigade. In 1890 the brigade acquired stables in Bishop Street and he transferred from the Highways and Sewage Department to the Fire Brigade on 10 March that year as the Brigade's horse keeper and coachman. Over the years he progressed through the ranks until in May 1916 he became 2nd Officer (deputy) to Henry Neal. Walter Parker retired at the end of September 1929 at the age of sixty. (M. Tovey)

Born at Coalville in the late nineteenth century, Arthur Cramp spent fourteen years as a glass artist and lead glazier before joining the Leicester Borough Fire Brigade in April 1912. Rising through the ranks, he was promoted to Second Officer (Deputy Chief) in 1929. Following the creation of the wartime National Fire Service he was appointed officer in charge of the Leicester Division, No. 9 Fire Area (Leicestershire and Northants), in September 1941. During the subsequent blitz he led a fire-fighting convoy made up of sections from Leicester, Nottingham, Derby and Chesterfield to Liverpool to assist in fighting the dockland fires which resulted from the heavy bombing suffered. A target for enemy aircraft attempting to prevent them from reaching the city, the convoy was heavily attacked on its journey and lost two appliances. From Liverpool, Cramp's contingent of fifteen pumps and eighty men was sent by destroyer to Belfast to give further aid to brigades there. Having served in the Leicester City Fire Brigade for thirty-three years Arthur Cramp retired in September 1945. (M. Tovey)

Officers and men of the Leicester City Fire Brigade in 1937. In July 1927 the brigade relocated from Rutland Street to purpose-built headquarters at Lancaster Place. This picture is probably taken to commemorate the retirement of Chief Officer Henry Neal. Front row, left to right: -?-, -?-, Station Officer Walter Sturgess, Visiting Officer Clarke, 2nd Officer Arthur Cramp, Chief Officer Henry Neal, 3rd Officer Farmer, -?-, -?-, -?-. (M. Tovey)

An aerial view of Lancaster Road fire station, 1973. *(Courtesy of the Urban Design Group, Leicester City Council)*

Sunday morning exercises on the Lancaster Road forecourt of the present headquarters. *(Author)*

Opposite, bottom: The old Guildhall, now a museum, was between 1836 and 1876 the Town Hall. The roadway was called Town Hall Lane and housed the police/fire station. *(Author)*

Superintendent Frederick Goodyer was the first Head Constable of the Leicester Borough Police Force when it was formed in January 1836. Goodyer came to Leicester from the newly formed Metropolitan Police and remained for only three years before in 1839 leaving to become the first Chief Constable of Leicestershire County Police. *(Courtesy of the Leicestershire Constabulary)*

Two of the biggest men to serve in the old Borough and City Police Force, both well known characters around the town, PC 83 John 'Tubby' Stephens (left), and Sgt 27 George Hankinson. 'Tubby' Stephens joined the Borough Police in 1886 on his return from Africa where he had served in the Royal Artillery during the Zulu War of 1879. Weighing 24 stones he was at one time reputed to be the heaviest policeman in England. Serving for twenty-two years, he died at his home in Cobden Street on 4 April 1904. George Hankinson, also in excess of 21 stones and over 6ft tall, joined the force in June 1910 and other than a period in the armed services during the First World War when he won the Military Medal for gallantry, he remained a policeman until his retirement in January 1936. (G. Jordan)

Bassoonist PC Albert Sims, seen here in about 1905, joined the Borough Police in 1904 and retired having reached the rank of inspector in 1929. (N. Haines)

Founded in 1873, the Borough Police band featured regularly in concerts on parks across the town and at other functions for thirty-three years until its dissolution in 1906. In the centre of the picture (in the top hat) is the bandmaster John Smith. *(Author)*

The Belgrave sub-division of the Leicester Borough Police, photographed between 1906 and 1908. The officer in charge on the front row wearing a military style pill-box cap is Superintendent John Thomas Noton. *(Courtesy of the Leicestershire Constabulary)*

Leicester Market Place, September 1912. The occasion is the award of medals in recognition of the coronation of King George V by Mayor Arthur Tollington to Borough Police officers. On the front row, looking towards the camera, is Superintendent Challis Hircock. In the background can be seen the façade of Simpkin and James' grocery store – regarded as one of the town's most élite shops throughout the 160 years that they occupied the site until economic change forced their closure at the end of 1970. *(Author)*

Officers of the North Evington sub-division between December 1928 and February 1929. Back row, left to right: PC Sheppard, PC Garfield, PC Bailey, PC Fraser, PC Warner. Middle row: PC Merriken (kia, Second World War, Royal Navy), PC Perkins, PC Newberry, PC Meese (later Chief Inspector), PC Ecob (later Deputy Chief Constable), PC Kirby, PC Leeson, PC Vines, PC Cross. Front row: PC Burton, -?-, Sgt Staines, Div. Inspector Faulkner, Sgt Buckby, PC Nutting, PC Matthews. *(Courtesy of the Leicestershire Constabulary)*

4   *Things are Looking Up*

The average passer-by, concentrating on making their way to a destination in any city centre rarely lifts their eyes above the level of the number on a door, or the name on a brass plate. Even when taking a casual stroll or on a shopping trip, it is the shop windows and displays at ground level that take one's attention.

This is an unfortunate, if understandable situation, which sadly deprives many people of a view of the ornamentation which adorn so many buildings and gable ends. Throughout the city at various locations, buildings erected a hundred years ago carry the evidence of builders' and architects' imagination in different ways. On occasion, as with the two rows of ceramic tiles along the front of the Thomas Cook building in Gallowtree Gate next to the Clock Tower, this takes the form of a pictorial tribute to the firm's past activities. Further along, in the High Street near to the junction of Cart's Lane, the old firm of Butler's who had a chemist shop on the corner, is the large picture of an apothecary mixing his potion above an advertisement for Butlers 'Sea Breezes' headache remedy. Elsewhere tradesmen's names and advertisements for 'bed and breakfast' can be seen painted over doorways and on chimney gables.

Further up the High Street, this time in celebration of the virtues of Empire, running along the façade of Arthur Wakerley's 'Singer Building', can be seen a series of cameos each depicting an animal representing a Commonwealth country, surmounting a flag of the British Empire.

A particularly unusual sight is the depiction of a Welshman, Englishman, Irishman and Scotsman in the moulded brickwork of a factory in Britannia Street. Historically (at the time the factory was built), this was an extremely poor district of lodging houses and rookeries.

On the outskirts of the city at Clarendon Park, Aylestone and Narborough Road, a different art form can be seen on the end walls of private houses or business premises – adverts for different trades and wares. Unlike those in the city centre, in the suburbs the paintings are much more modern, sometimes (as in the 'Sid Mottram' advert), being as recent as the early 1960s.

Photographed during the early part of the twentieth century, this view shows a 1904 open-top tramcar travelling into the town along High Street, passing the Singer Sewing Machine Company's impressive façade towards Cart's Lane. Annal's drapers and ladies' outfitters shop on the left at 56 High Street was taken over between 1914 and 1922 by the Leicester Co-op butchery department. *(Courtesy of the Midlands Co-operative Society)*

An almost identical shot taken a century later. The tramcars have now gone although the row of buildings is little changed. While the name 'Butler's' has now been removed from the stonework between the first- and second-storey windows, the 'apothecary tiles' further along the façade over High Street are still in pristine condition. *(Author)*

The apothecary tiles, still looking impressive after many years of gracing the façade of the building.

The lead inscription on the Butler's building, featuring the apothcaries' pestle and mortar.

The original Thomas Cook building with the frieze depicting part of the company's history between 1841 and 1894 running along the front at second- and third-floor levels. *(Author)*

Thomas Cook (1808–92) was born in Derbyshire and initially served an apprenticeship as a cabinet maker. A devout temperance worker, in 1841 he conceived the idea of running a Temperance Society trip from Leicester to Loughborough on the Midland Railway line at a price of 1s per head including refreshments. Following this he established his own business running rail excursions offering trips to Scotland, and eventually to destinations all over the world. *(Courtesy of the Thomas Cook Archives)*

The attractive frieze which adorns the Thomas Cook building. *(Author)*

Pictured in about 1970, these long-forgotten stables in Rutland Street are evocative of a bygone era. Although the name of the proprietor is too faded to be distinguishable, it can still be seen that the hackmaster who owned the premises, hired out 'Victorias, Traps, Brakes & Charabancs' drawn by a selection of 'Greys and Bays'. Additional services offered were transport for weddings and furniture removals. *(E. Selvidge)*

Designed by Arthur Wakerley, the Turkey Café on Granby Street (opposite Bishop Street), is another fine example of what can be seen along the upper levels of buildings in the city centre. Designed as a replica of Turkish architecture, the main motif is picked out in vibrant red, blue, green, and gold mosaics. *(Author)*

Churchgate in the days before the development of the Shires shopping centre. Painted on the brickwork at second-floor level over the premises of May's electrical shop, and probably dating back to the inter-war years, is a sign offering bed and breakfast for *2s 6d*. *(E. Selvidge)*

Look to the rooftops in the Market Place and you will see a remnant of a bygone era. Long-gone drapers, Grant's Linen House, had an advertisement just below chimney level. Viewed here from the top of Victoria Parade is the block of buildings in which the old Gaumont Cinema used to stand. *(Author)*

Hardly touched by the years, this advert in the Narborough Road district was probably created as late as the 1960s. *(Author)*

This advert for Allard's Stores in Highfield Street has sadly been damaged by the removal of the right-hand side of the text. Picked out in vibrant colours, the artwork is in almost pristine condition. *(Author)*

Throughout the nineteenth century the Belgrave district of Leicester was infamous for being the roughest area of the town with migrant Irish workers living in lodging houses and rookeries across the district and up into Abbey Street. Britannia Street, seen here in later years, was in the heart of the district. Even areas such as this possessed their small idiosyncrasies which can be discerned in the chased-out brickwork over the first floor of the factory in the centre of the picture, representing an Englishman, Irishman, Welshman and Scotsman (detailed close-ups below, and below, opposite). *(Author)*

In September 1880 two converted cottages in Woodboy Street
(next to Britannia Street) were purchased by the Watch
Committee and a branch police station opened under the
command of Inspector Hickinbottom (right), who paid *2s 6d* per
week rent with free gas and coal on the proviso that his wife was
to keep the station and cells clean. In 1930 the station became
home to the first city Police Force's first traffic department with
six officers and a mechanic. (*Author*)

Built by the prominent Victorian architect Arthur Wakerley, the Singer Building (also known as Coronation, and the Jubilee Buildings) at 76–88 High Street is probably most renowned for the carvings of animals which adorn its façade at third-floor level. Depicting the dominions of the British Empire they present a fascinating insight into Victorian perceptions. There is a variation to present-day usage in the one of the elephants depicting Burma, which is spelt 'Burmah'. (*Author*)

5   *Established Businesses*

In the post-war years many of Leicester's long-established firms based in what had always been seen to be the 'stable industries', found themselves in difficulties, or were simply bought out and absorbed by larger, more anonymous, parent companies. The situation was not necessarily peculiar to Leicester (although some of the ingredients in the process locally, such as an over abundance of labour in relation to job vacancies was). Nationwide there was a huge economic slide during the 1970s which resulted in the failure of businesses across the country.

Historically, Leicester relied very much on the hosiery trade along with the boot and shoe manufacturing industry. Both of these lost a huge amount of ground after 1945 in the face of cheaper goods being imported from across the world. However many firms outside of this sphere survived the economic depression and are still very much 'alive and well' in the twenty-first century. A few of these companies, all of whom are household names within the town and county, are shown here with details of their origins and background.

Built in 1899 on the outskirts of the town at Knighton Fields Road East, in its prime the Co-operative Society's Wheatsheaf factory was one of the largest shoe production sites in Europe. A victim of a post-war economic decline, the factory finally closed down in 1990, just eight years before reaching its centenary. *(Courtesy of the Midlands Co-operative Society)*

Ralph Rossa, the founder of R. Rossa & Sons, ice cream manufacturers. Rafael Boccarossa came to England at the turn of the twentieth century from his native province of Frosinone in Italy. Settling in Leicester, he bought from his uncle, Feretti Boccarossa, a small ice cream business based at 45 Bedford Street. Joined later by his sons Don and Antonio and shortening his first name to Ralph and the family name to 'Rossa' he created one of the major ice cream companies in the city, producing traditional Italian ice cream. Following his untimely death from a stroke in 1961 at the age of 77, Ralph Rossa's sons, Don and Antonio, (Toni), took over the business. (I am indebted for the background information on the company of R. Rossa & Sons, to the founder's grandchildren Justina Fewkes and Gary Rossa). *(Courtesy of R. Rossa & Sons)*

Sometime during the 1920s Ralph Rossa was responsible for the creation in what is now Middleton Street, (then known as Union Street or Coalpit Lane), of the Japanese Gardens at Aylestone. Not a lot, other than personal recollections remain to either date or exactly locate these gardens other than that they were a place for public recreation and that a bandstand provided music for tea dances. As Ralph Rossa served in the British Army during the First World War, the project could not have been begun by him until after 1919 and the gardens had ceased to exist by 1935 when Justina Marcantonio, his granddaughter, came to Leicester. Seen here at the time of construction are, from left to right: Ralph Boccarossa, his cousin Feretti who owned the 'Venetian Rooms' in Churchgate, Don Rossa, Enrico Fattarolli (Ralph's brother-in-law and owner of 'Eric's Ice Creams'), another major ice cream manufacturer in the city. The building in the background with the timbered gable is the Union Inn on Middleton Street. *(Courtesy of R. Rossa & Sons)*

Resting in the yard on a summer's day between the wars at 45 Bedford Street is Walter Young with some ice cream barrels, flanked by Toni and Don Rossa. The company moved in 1943 to its present location in Stonebridge Street. *(Courtesy of R. Rossa & Sons)*

Two unidentified
ladies enjoying a
cornet at the
Japanese
Gardens, 1920s.
*(Courtesy of R.
Rossa & Sons)*

Don Rossa (1907–88), left, who with his
brother Toni took over the business after the
death of Ralph Rossa and who himself was
succeeded by his sons Gary (pictured above),
and his brother Malcolm. *(Courtesy of
R. Rossa & Sons)*

Over the years the company progressed from horse-drawn carts (the company had four horses which were stabled near to the Bedford Street premises) to motorised vans which covered the outlying council estates. *(Courtesy of R. Rossa & Sons)*

Stibbe's factory in Great Central Street, 1984. Once one of the city's major employers, Stibbe's became overstretched during the 1970s in the 'double jersey boom' which brought down many companies when the bubble burst. The notice on the front of the building bears the simple message, 'TO LET 150,000 square feet of modern factory space'. *(E.R. Welford)*

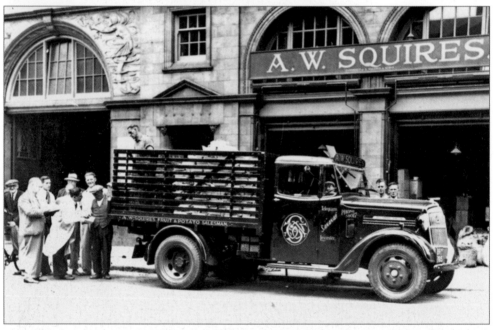

The wholesale fruit and vegetable market in Halford Street was for many years the central purchasing area for fruiterers and greengrocers throughout the city. In 1962, following discussions to move it to Southampton Street, a proposition was made to the Markets Committee that a new site occupying some 105,000sq yds should be created on Freemen's Common. The Chairmen of the Leicester Wholesale Fruit Market Ltd., P.M. Lister and J.M. Squires subsequently went to view existing markets in Belgium, France and Germany before making recommendations on the layout of the new development. Work on Freemen's Common began in June 1967 and just over twelve months later, on 5 October 1968, the old market closed down, though the fish market section remained open for some time after this. The brand new Reo Speedwagon lorry seen here during the inter-war years is being loaded outside Squires' premises. It was supplied by the Leicester firm of Douglas Weir who were based in Fleetwood Road before moving to Welford Road, and bears the telephone number '58017' – and reminiscent of the times, the information that telegrams should be sent to 'SANANAB, Leicester'. *(C. Chesterman)*

Throughout the 1950s and '60s, N. Corah & Sons Ltd, was one of the most prosperous hosiery manufacturers in the country. it expanded its Leicester base at St Margaret's Works, and bought other sites in Rochdale, Barnsley and Scunthorpe. However, with the recession biting, by the mid-1970s they announced redundancies and a shorter working

week, and eventually, in common with many other Leicester hosiery firms, by the turn of the twenty-first century they had closed. *(C. Chesterman)*

Beginning business in 1932 on Saffron Lane, H.T.H. Peck moved into the impressive building at West Bridge in 1949, where they employed 900 workers and traded as 'Pex Socks and Stockings'. They became one of the nation's largest producers of women's fully fashioned stockings. By the early 1990s the firm was announcing cut-backs, and ceased manufacturing in October 1999. The building on West Bridge was originally built in about 1844 as a factory for J. Whitmore & Sons, Worsted Spinners. In 1932 Whitmore's was acquired by Paton & Baldwin Ltd. Following the demise of Peck's, the factory was redeveloped and taken over by the Land Registry Department. *(M. Ford)*

One of the longest-established companies in Leicester is Everard's Brewery. Founded in 1849 by William Everard in Southgates, the company expanded rapidly and subsequently set up a chain of public houses in the area. In 1875 the building pictured here, the Castle Street Brewery, replaced the original one. Just before the turn of the twentieth century in 1892 they moved part of their operation to Burton upon Trent in order to take advantage of the famed Burton water and in 1932 Everards closed the Leicester Brewery, and production moved to the Tiger Brewery in Burton. During 1985 brewing was recommenced in Leicestershire at the new purpose-built Castle Acres Brewery near Narborough, and in 1990 all Everards Ales were once again brewed in Leicestershire when the Burton Brewery finally ceased production. The solid-tyre drays shown here outside the Castle Street brewery are Sentinel steam wagons, and date to the inter-war years – probably the 1920s. *(Courtesy of Everards Brewery)*

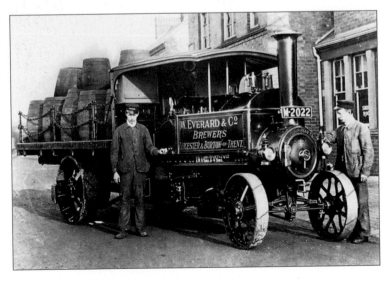

A very early example of a mechanical dray belonging to 'W. Everard & Co., Brewers, Leicester & Burton-on-Trent'. Judging by the registration number of the vehicle this image can be dated to about the first decade of the twentieth century. *(Courtesy of Everards Brewery)*

William Everard, the founder of Everard's Brewery in 1849. (*Courtesy of Everards Brewery*)

Chairman of Everard's since 1988, Richard Everard DL, Master of the Worshipful Company of Brewers 2004–5. By the beginning of the twenty-first century the company had become one of a major employer owning 161 pubs in eleven counties and producing around 18.7 million pints of beer a year. (*Courtesy of Everards Brewery*)

GIVING A PARTY?

You can rely upon

EVERARDS

"*Gentlemen - The Best!*"

From all **OFF LICENCES SHOWING THIS SIGN** or any **EVERARDS HOUSE**

Or if you desire it direct from SOUTHGATE BREWERY, LEICESTER
Telephone 20727 (3 lines)

A FEW SUGGESTIONS

NUT BROWN ALE	....	14 6 per doz. large
LIGHT BURTON (a pale dinner ale)	14 6 per doz. large
NUT BROWN ALE	....	7 9 per doz. small
INDIA PALE ALE (Burton brewed)	11 6 per doz. small
OLD BILL'S BREW	....	10 6 per doz. small
BARLEY WINE STRONG ALE
(Gold medal)	16 6 per doz. nips

Guinness Stout, Extra Stout, Hammerton Oatmeal Stout, etc
at competitive prices

ORDERS OF 1 DOZ LARGE UPWARDS DELIVERED FREE

An Everard's soft drinks lorry, 1954. (*C. Chesterman*)

Left: The famous 'Gentlemen the Best', poster which became for many years the slogan of Everard's. In the early 1950s, before the advent of supermarkets and other retail outlets, most pubs still maintained an 'off-sales' shop from which bottled and draught beers could be bought for home consumption. (*Courtesy of Everards Brewery*)

Two views of the Southgates and underpass area of the city showing different views of the old brewery before it was finally closed down in 1982. The first shows the cathedral and its grounds with the nearby Castle Court set next to the Judge's Lodgings. At the bottom left is the H.T.H. Peck's factory, later to be developed and passed over for use as the Land Registry Offices. The second presents an aerial shot of the underpass taking traffic beneath St Nicholas Circle. *(E. Selvidge)*

Anyone who is familiar with the present Marquis Wellington at 139 London Road could be excused for failing to spot it on this picture. It is in the block of small terraced houses between the man walking down London Road, and the two gentlemen studying the billboards outside Kempin's tobacconist shop. The photograph, taken between 1901 and 1904, shows the horse tramlines in the road which were soon to be replaced by ornate central tram standards carrying the overhead wires for the electric tramcars that would run along London Road to Stoneygate after May 1904. *(Courtesy of Everards Brewery)*

Taken from almost the same spot just over a hundred years later, the entire row of properties has changed. The ornate bow-fronted Marquis Wellington is not recognisable as the old property, and has encroached to include Johnson & Sons at no. 141. The church which stood at the junction of Victoria (later University) Road is now the Seventh-Day Adventist Church. Kempin's shop has been replaced by the Fraser Noble Building, belonging to Leicester University. A notable remaining feature is the stone gatepost to the church at the right-hand corner. *(Author)*

The first coach to be operated by G.H. Woods, seen in 1950 outside the family home in Marstown Avenue at Wigston. *(Courtesy of Woods Coaches & J. Breen)*

Woods Coaches began its operation from a garage on Kenilworth Road before the development of the area. It is seen here in 1958. *(Courtesy of Woods Coaches & J.Breen)*

Below: Mark Wood, Chairman of Wood's Coaches. *Right:* George Wood, (1919–2000). Begun in 1949 by George Wood with one coach in a garage on Kenilworth Road allotments at Wigston, Wood's Coaches is now one of the largest independently owned travel firms in the Midlands. During 1963 the company moved to its present vehicle depot and offices site in Bedford Road on the Fairfield Estate. In 1967 George Wood's son Mark joined the firm as a director, and later became chairman of the company. Remaining a family business Wood's now employ nearly a hundred people and in addition to a fleet of mini-buses operating across the city, their fleet of thirteen luxury coaches run on tour routes across Great Britain and Europe. *(Courtesy of Woods Coaches)*

Boots chemist shop at 136 Hinckley Road, early 1950s. This store was removed during the middle of that decade to a new site nearby at 227 Hinckley Road. *(Courtesy of the Boots Archive)*

Before its closure, the Narborough Road store at the junction of Norman Street was a well-known local landmark. *(Courtesy of the Boots Archive)*

One of Leicester's most famous landmarks, the Statue of Liberty stood on top of the Lowe & Carr building in Walnut Street until, having been disposed of just before the turn of the twenty-first century, it was converted into an apartment building. The structure was originally commissioned by Samuel Lennard, (1851–1901), a shoe factor in nearby Asylum Street. Liberty Shoes, founded in 1900 by Disney Charles Barlow and Sir Samuel Briers (also trading from Asylum Street), moved into the premises in 1921. Erected in the same year, the statue was based on F.A. Barthold's Statue of Liberty in New York Harbour. This version is probably the work of Liverpool-born sculptor Herbert Morcom (1871–1942), who decorated many Leicester buildings while he was

teaching at Leicester College of Art between 1910 and 1935. The factory itself was designed by Exeter-born architect Howard Henry Thomson (c. 1887–1922) who, having come to Leicester in 1887 as assistant to Arthur Wakerley, established his own practice at 8 Market Street from 1904. Liberty Shoes closed down in 1962 when the building was taken over by the printing firm of Lowe & Carr. (Top: G. Fenn; left: E.R. Welford; bottom: Author)

Cutting timber at Sanvey Gate sawmill
during the 1940s. *(G. Fenn)*

Before being absorbed into the Raab Kärcher Group during the latter part of the twentieth
century, the firm of Gimson & Sons was one of the oldest established businesses in Leicester.
Its founder William Gimson began trading (first as a carpenter and then as a timber
merchant) in 1834 from his premises at 47 Welford Road. Before the turn of the twentieth
century the company also owned an extensive sawing and planing mill in Sanvey Gate, and
was also making specialist cigar boxes for the numerous manufacturers in the borough.
Later, during the mid-1950s, the extensive Swan Lake Mills site on Upperton Road became
the company's main trading base, attracting visits from personalities such as Larry Grayson
in 1989. Also the company were at the forefront in the supplying sectional buildings,
popular in the 1990s, to the building trade. During the first decade of the twenty-first
century the site was acquired by Barratt Developments to become the location of the
'Freemen's Meadow' housing project. *(G. Fenn)*

Having been developed after the war into an extensive industrial base for firms such as Gimson's timber yard (later Raab Kärcher) and Mawby & King the glass merchants, by 2005 the site was once again undergoing a change of use, this time as part of a regeneration of the Eastern Boulevard area, into an area of high-class dwellings. *(Author)*

One of the oldest pubs in Leicester city centre is the Globe at 43 Silver Street. Seen here during the first decade of the twentieth century, probably sometime between 1903 and 1909, the picture portrays the atmosphere of a summer's day in the years before the First World War. Written on the glass of the lamp outside the door is the name of the licensee, Joe Noble. *(Courtesy of Everard's Brewery)*

6   Seen from the Air

The changes across the city centre and its environs since the Second World War have been considerable. New buildings have been added and the construction of the ring road system has altered the view somewhat. Looking at Leicester from the air, mainly in the early and mid-1970s, most of these additions and changes can be seen, and this is probably an optimum period to look at much of the finished work of the post-war planners before those of the late twentieth century began once more to put their stamp on things.

Developments on the outskirts at locations such as Braunstone Aerodrome resulted in new industrial estates housing companies such as Fox's Confectionery and Charles Clore's British Shoe Corporation. In later years this philosophy was further broadened with the opening of the Fosse Park and Grove Farm Park sites at junction 21 of the M1. One or two locations have changed little in structure, but considerably in usage; for instance Clarendon Park district, always a busy shopping area, has become very much a café and restaurant location.

The views shown on these pages depict a totally different picture of Leicester to that which a Victorian or Edwardian occupant would have recognised. In the thirty-odd years since they were photographed, current changes and developments in the overall structure and layout of the city have produced yet further significant differences once more altering its aspect.

Taken in July or August 1973, this photograph gives a unique view of the of the city from the west. Beginning at the lower right, with West Bridge running past the old factory building of H.T.H. Peck [1] backing onto the Grand Union Canal (in 1997 this was to become the Land Registry Office), to the distinctive profile of St Nicholas Circle with its impressive Holiday Inn Hotel [2] and the Southgates underpass [3] (built between August 1966 and May 1968), taking traffic beneath. Following the line of the underpass through into Burley's Way, the St Margaret's Swimming Baths [4] complex (opened 1966) is shown on the right, before passing St Margaret's Bus Station [5] opposite Corah's St Margaret's Works [6]. Thames Tower [7] (built in 1970) at seventeen storeys high, once the tallest building on the city skyline features in the top left quadrant.

Working towards the Clock Tower and the Haymarket Centre [8] (completed 1973) there still remains a view of the High Street area before its face was irrevocably altered a few years later by the construction of the Shires shopping centre. Notably still in existence at this time is the massive Fielding Johnson factory in East Bond Street [9] opposite to St Peter's car park [10] which was demolished in 2006 as part of the John Lewis development. In front of Leicester's first multi-storey car park in Lee Circle [11] (opened in December 1961) situated on Charles Street is Epic House [12] one-time home to Radio Leicester, while at the top right can be seen the Charnwood Estate project [13] and the LMS Railway yards [14]. *(Courtesy of the Urban Design Group, Leicester City Council)*

A bird's-eye view of the Leicester University complex in the mid-1970s with Victoria Park in the background. During the First World War the disused buildings of the old County Lunatic Asylum were taken over by the military and used to create one of the biggest war hospitals (the 5th Northern General) in the Midlands. With the last patient due to be discharged in September 1919, the City Council were examining plans for the creation of a university when Thomas Fielding Johnson, a wealthy local businessman, announced that he had purchased the site and proposed to donate it to the city for the establishing of a university in April of that year. *(Courtesy of the Urban Design Group, Leicester City Council)*

Opposite: Taken soon after opening of the Misterton to Markfield stretch of the M1 motorway in January 1965, this picture shows the disused Braunstone Aerodrome. The building between the road and the motorway is the Airman's Rest pub. Since the turn of the twentieth century Fox's had been a substantial employer in the city. Run as a family business, Eric, the son of the founder, Walter Fox, had developed the 'Fox's Glacier Mint', a clear peppermint sweet which, advertised by the cartoon figure of 'Peppy the Polar Bear', shot the company to international fame by the end of the First War. Following the loss of their premises in Oxford Street owing to redevelopment in 1960, the company moved to this new purpose-built site at Braunstone. *(Top: E. Selvidge; middle and bottom: Courtesy of Fox's Confectionery)*

Built on the outskirts of the city on 51 acres of agricultural land purchased in 1954, County Hall, the county administration centre for Leicestershire County Council opened at Glenfield in November 1967. *(E. Selvidge)*

Opposite, top: Seen here are Parker Drive and the old stadium that was used for many years as a greyhound racing and motorcycle speedway track. Opposite the stadium is the factory of Bentley's which prior to the liquidation of the company and its subsidiaries in April 1988 with outstanding debts of £7 million was one of the city's major employers. *(E. Selvidge)*

Opposite, bottom: A coach belonging to Swinfield's Tours waits outside of the main grandstand entrance in Parker Drive to pick up a party from the stadium in the early 1950s. *(C. Chesterman)*

In the centre of this picture dating from summer 1973 is the 2-acre site which accommodates the twin office blocks that in 1975 were to become the subject of contention when the City Council was split over their purchase for use as the New Walk Centre. In the top right is still to be seen Hillcrest Hospital and the newly constructed tower blocks of the St Peter's Estate. At the bottom left is Gateway School and the College of Art and Technology (later De Montfort University). *(Urban Design Group, Leicester City Council)*

Standing forlorn at the intersection of the new gyratory system is the ancient Magazine Arch. It was left deliberately by John Beckett, the architect of the new road systems before his retirement in 1964, as an alternative to building a traffic island. Midland Red buses can still be seen waiting at stands in what was the old Newarke Bus Station. The Cathedral and Castle Gardens run down to join the canal at the bottom left, while at the top there is a clear view of the BT telephone exchange, Wharf Street. *(Urban Design Group, Leicester City Council)*

The structure remarkably resembling an egg box at the centre of the picture is in fact the newly installed prefabricated roofing of the retail market, with the imposing Corn Exchange to one side. Although the ground to the rear of the Corn Exchange has been cleared, at this time work had not commenced on the retail hall that was to house the Fish and Meat Market. (*Urban Design Group, Leicester City Council*)

Towards the bottom half of the picture is an as yet undeveloped St Margaret's bus station, which has still to covered in. Seen in the mid-1970s, on the right is an excellent view of the area of streets (marked particularly by the Fielding Johnson Works), that was later in its initial development to become the Shires shopping centre. In the first decade of the twenty-first century, along with the John Lewis development this would dominate the entire block from High Street to Burley's Way. The elliptical shape of the top deck of St Peter's car park, demolished in 2005/6, is very clear at the far right. In the top right corner, sitting on the Y-shaped junction of Welford and Aylestone roads, is the now-demolished Granby Halls, with the Leicester Tigers rugby ground behind it. *(Urban Design Group, Leicester City Council)*

Probably the most prominent building here is the box-like shape of the Holiday Inn facing West Bridge. Immediately to its right is what remains of the Castle Street and Redcross Street area dominated by Everard's Brewery. Looking from the Holiday Inn to the middle of the picture is an area of cleared and shuttered ground opposite to St Nicholas Place which, in 2005, became the home of Radio Leicester. *(Urban Design Group, Leicester City Council)*

Seen from the air in about 1976, opposite Granby Halls and along Walnut Street still stand the houses that were due to be demolished when the Leicester Royal Infirmary extension work and car park were commenced. (There is an area of ground behind them cleared in readiness). Founded in 1891 as Leicester Fosse, the Filbert Street ground (bottom left) was home to Leicester City Football Club until its move in 2002 to the nearby Walker's Stadium. *(E. Selvidge)*

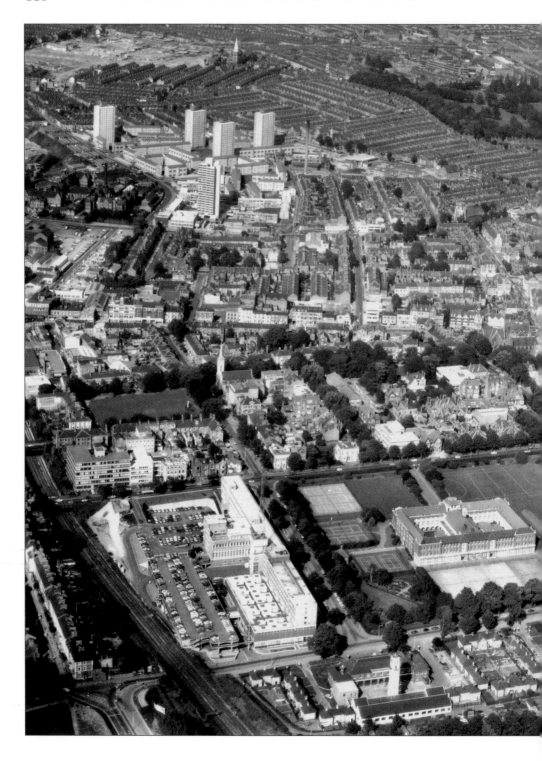

Approaching the city from the south side, this picture shows the large amount of ground occupied by the old Wyggeston Girls' School in the 1970s. The line of trees running across the centre shows the line of new Walk, while to the right is De Montfort Hall at the edge of Victoria Park, with the pavilion just above the tennis courts. *(Urban Design Group, Leicester City Council)*

Laid out in the pincer-like jaws between Victoria Park and Queen's roads, Clarendon Park, on the southern border of the city, has changed little over the years. Large, imposing houses face onto Victoria Park backed by a network of closely packed side-streets. The tall tower block to the right of the picture is St Leonard's Court, a block of flats at the corner of St Leonard's and Victoria Park roads. Now very much a shopping and bistro area, the majority of these streets were in the latter part of the twentieth century partially blocked off and designated one-way to restrict traffic flow. *(E. Selvidge)*

7 Later Years

During the latter years of the twentieth century, work continued to complete the long-term plans laid down by city councillors such as Charles Keene and his Reconstruction Committee, in collaboration with City Surveyor John Beckett. These were first outlined in the 'Fifty Year' development plan for Leicester. Towards the end of this work, others such as the town's first Planning Officer, Konrad Smigielski, added their own touches, and the ground was laid for future developers to take the city into the twenty-first century. While new shopping areas such as the Shires, and St Martin's were constructed around the actual centre, in other places historic features were unfortunately lost. The majority of the properties along Southgate Street, including such buildings as the old Blue Boar Inn, and the Magazine barracks were razed to provide a route for the new ring road and the Southgates underpass. On the other side of the city on the edge of the Highfields district, Hillcrest Hospital (renamed in a vain attempt to obliterate its original purpose and image – originally the town's workhouse), along with all of its history was lost in the name of progress in order to make room for the Moat Community College. Other features such as Granby Halls and the cattle market also disappeared soon after the turn of the twenty-first century.

Elsewhere, along the canal bank from West Bridge down to the power station, areas such as Swan Lake Mills (now Freemen's Meadows) and Bede Island have been transformed into attractive complexes of multi-occupation dwellings. Commercially, in a move to persuade shoppers away from the city centre, a conurbation of retail outlets has been created on the southern outskirts of the city near to the M1.

Designed by William Parsons (1797–1857) and built as the Union Workhouse in 1839, Hillcrest Hospital closed on 21 November 1975 and was demolished in October 1977 to make way for Moat Community College which presently occupies the site. With its main entrance on Swain Street, Hillcrest had a lesser known access through a small wicket door in Upper Conduit Street near to the garages (now Maidstone Road), which gave access to the lodging house accommodation – better known as 'the Spike'. In this part of the building, vagrants, on production of a signed authorisation (a 'Spike ticket' issued at the central police station), were allowed to sleep for a maximum of three consecutive nights. Originally designed to accommodate 800 people, in 1862 an extension was added to the north elevation in order to house a further 100 inhabitants and to provide a workhouse school. In 1886 two new infirmary blocks were added along with a nurses' home and dispensary. These later became the women's hospital. Towards the end of the First World War a short-lived experiment was conducted to utilise the old hospital as an auxiliary unit to the 5th Northern General Hospital for wounded soldiers being brought back from France. Opening on 21 July 1918 it was closed down on 11 December that year. Even the War Office had to concede that it was unacceptable to return men from the rigours of the trenches and put them into the workhouse. (*Photograph courtesy of the Urban Design Group, Leicester City Council; the author is indebted to Derek Seaton for his assistance identifying the various buildings within the hospital complex*)

KEY
1 Male hospital, (3 wards)
2 Female house
3 Offices & Committee room
4 Deputy Supt's., residence
5 Lodge
6 Nurses home
7 Female hospital (6 wards)
8 Bake house
9 Mortuary
10 Male house
11 Boiler house
12 Garages
13 Upper Conduit St. (Maidstone Rd.)
14 Sparkenhoe St.
15 LMS railway
16 Hutchinson Walk

Below: In September 1990 the initial stages of work were carried out on the Shires shopping centre project. *(E.R. Welford)*

Seen here in 1984, the Granby Halls were built in 1915 as the Junior Training Hall for the purposes of preparing recruits for the army. Before its demolition in October 2000 it was used variously as a trade exhibition centre, wrestling venue and roller-skating rink. (*E.R. Welford*)

Plans for a new cattle market on Aylestone Road to replace the site in Horsefair Street (which was required for the erection of the proposed 'New Town Hall'), were approved in 1871. Work was quickly put in hand, and the new cattle market – occupying the ground between Welford Road and Aylestone Road – was opened on 6 April 1872. A prosperous farmers' market remained there until well into the twentieth century. Its peak year being 1966, when 171,572 animals went though its pens. The market's last auction was held in December 1988, after which, following the development of the ground for commercial purposes, the supermarket firm Safeway constructed a store. In March 2004, Morrison's bought out Safeway to create the fourth-largest supermarket chain in the UK. Seen here, Morrison's now occupies the ground facing the old market clock, and the present-day car park is situated where the old cattle pens once stood. (*Top: G. Fenn; bottom: Author*)

As part of the road and bridge-widening scheme to improve traffic flow into and out of the city on its western approaches from Hinckley Road, the railway bridge and properties at the junction with Corah Street are seen here in the process of demolition, March 1984. (E.R. Welford)

Opened in July 1938 just before the Second World War, the Odeon Cinema in Rutland Street survived many of its contemporaries including the Picture House, the Essoldo, the Savoy (ABC) and the Gaumont all of which succumbed to the new age of television and home video. Its demise could not be postponed indefinitely and soon after the turn of the twenty-first century it became a conference and banqueting centre. *(E.R. Welford)*

Begun in 1984, the Caribbean Carnival, celebrating Leicester's Afro-Caribbean community, has become an annual one-day event, held in August each year. The pictures here are taken from the 1986 celebrations. *(Author)*

The power station. *(G. Fenn)*

With the end of the First World War in sight, in October 1917 Leicester Corporation purchased 35 acres of ground on the Freemen's Meadows and at a projected cost of £250,000, put in hand the building of a new power station bounded by Aylestone Road, St Mary's Road and the Rawdykes, to supply the needs of the borough. The power station remained in operation until almost the end of the century, when following the demolition of its trademark cooling towers, the ground was eventually developed by Leicester City Football Club as the new Walker's Stadium. (The four central towers were scheduled for demolition on Sunday 3 July 1983. While the two middle towers collapsed as planned, the outer ones did not and had to be brought down the following morning with a hawser attached to a tractor which cut around the base in a similar manner to a cheese-wire). (*Author*)

On 29 July 1981 in common with cities across the United Kingdom, street parties were held throughout Leicester in celebration of the marriage of HRH Prince Charles to Lady Diana Spencer. Seen here at one of the many, Radio Leicester presenter Mike Smith provides the entertainment. The banner in the background of the top photograph proclaims this to be 'The Fresh Brew Tea Party'.
(*Radio Leicester*)

In 1984 the early stages of another shopping development were underway, this time the
St Martins project at the back of Cank Street. *(E.R. Welford)*

St Martin's
development.
(E.R. Welford)

During the 1980s Sikhs worldwide were involved in a movement to establish a national status for themselves (the Khalsa Panth), and a homeland – Khalistan – in India. Seen here on London Road, Leicester Sikhs, wearing the orange-coloured turban which was the symbol of the movement, are holding a march into the city centre during the summer of 1984. *(Author)*

In April 1984 at the height of the dispute between the National Union of Miners and the government, a group of thirty-one miners from Kent set out on a march from their home county to Nottingham. Having walked 185 miles in less than a week, they arrived at Leicester where, joined by a further hundred men from Yorkshire and South Wales, on Friday 13 April they continued along London Road from Victoria Park to Town Hall Square to hold a rally before embarking on the last leg of their journey. *(E.R. Welford)*

A victim of the building changes in the Sanvey Gate area, this old pub, the Duke of Cumberland, along with the neighbouring side street Elbow Lane, disappeared soon after the turn of the twenty-first century. *(E.R. Welford)*

Seen here in January 1986, the Spread Eagle, along with many of the adjacent properties fell under the auctioneer's hammer during 2006 and 2007. All that remains to identify the site is the post-box (in the right-hand inset) which stood outside in Charles Street. *(E.R. Welford & Author)*

Granted planning permission in January 1969, the St Peter's car park was built soon after the ones at Lee Circle and Abbey Street. It was demolished in 2006 as part of the John Lewis extension to the Shires shopping centre. *(E.R. Welford & Author)*

Causeway Lane, 2006. *(Author)*

The BT building, clad in polythene and seen from St George's Way in early 2007. The banner hanging on the side of the building proclaims: 'A £33 million regeneration providing 400,000sq. ft of landmark mixed use development'. *(Author)*

Built in 1933 as the Leicester City Police Headquarters the building is seen here from the rear in July 2006 in the process of being incorporated into the Colton Square property development. *(Author)*